I0635493

THE DRESSAGE JUDGE'S VIEWPOINT

CONTENTS

THE DRESSAGE JUDGE'S VIEWPOINT

This guide looks at dressage from the judge's point if view: what is involved in becoming a judge, and then becoming a better one, and what judges look for in the movements of the tests and the basic way of going.

Trainers and riders can learn from the judges' viewpoints, not just in the search for better marks in the arena, but also in the development of this very special sport of dressage. We need to break down any barriers between the different sectors of the sport as we can all learn so much from each other.

Judges, in turn, must remember that riders and trainers are more likely to be sympathetic to their viewpoint if it is positive and helpful rather than critical and petty. We judges need to look for what is good in a test and, to this end, in the section on Movements the emphasis is on what earns the marks. The things that lose marks are there to illuminate what is good by presenting the opposites rather than just listing the first things the judges look for.

Finally, honesty is fundamental to good judging, along with the confidence to give marks quickly and to be able to express good reasons for the assessment. But alongside confidence, humility is needed because all judges make mistakes in their demanding task, and even the best judges always have more to learn. One of the most exciting aspects of dressage judging is the never ending opportunity to learn from books, videos, other judges, riders, trainers and of course the horses.

THE WORK OF THE JUDGE

THE SHEETS

Test sheets list the movements of the test and usually give directives to the judges, riders and trainers as to what is required. Owning a set of test sheets is a good idea as you then have any test available as needed and have a reference with which to build up a complete picture of the movements required from the easiest levels (Preliminary) to the most difficult (Grand Prix).

The score sheet is divided into columns giving room for the marks and comments for each movement. At the bottom of the page are columns for the collective marks which assess the overall way of going as opposed to the technical requirements of the movements.

The scale of marks is in a box in one corner of the score sheet and the first requirement for any judge is to learn what each mark is in both words and figures. The easiest way of deciding the appropriate mark is asking yourself: 'Was it *Good?*' and if it was give an 8, but if only *Fairly good* give the 7. Occasionally you can ask yourself if it was *Very good* and be able to give the 9. Get into the habit of asking the question.

The scale of marks is as follows	
10. Excellent	4. Insufficient
9. Very good	3. Fairly bad
8. Good	2. Bad
7. Fairly good	1. Very bad
6. Satisfactory	0. Not performed
5. Sufficient	

Images The skill of judging is to build up clear images of the goal of each movement. Develop a clear picture of what is a *Very good* halt in a Novice test, a *Very good* free-rein walk, a *Very good* working trot circle and so on. If you prefer you could use images of *Excellent* examples, but the important thing is to watch training sessions and competitions and establish your own clear images.

TRAINING TO BE A JUDGE

RIDING THE MOVEMENTS

Another judging skill is building up a complete picture and understanding of what is happening. It is easy to identify one fault such as overbending, but the appropriate mark for this fault will depend on what else is happening. If the suppleness, impulsion and rhythm are all good then few marks will be lost. Seeing the complete picture and not just focusing on one fault is easier for those judges who have ridden the movements being judged.

WATCHING

Hours spent watching horses work will reap rewards for judging. It is invaluable for developing a real understanding of the training that teaches the horses to do the movements well and to display quality work in the arena.

SITTING IN

Listening to how other judges assess a class is a great education, so try to get permission to sit in with other judges in their car or judges' box.

PRACTISE JUDGING

Experience is an essential ingredient for improvement, so practise (with the permission of the organisers) with your own writer and sheets.

READING

There is a great deal of good material to help judges build up a sound theoretical basis for their decisions. The most important are the Federation Equestre Internationale (FEI) Directives which are published in the *British Dressage Rule Book* and these should be learned forwards, backwards and inside out. Then, of course, there is a mass of wonderful dressage books written by the great masters of each era from the seventeenth century to the present day.

PREPARATION FOR A TEST

LEARNING THE TEST

Judges have to learn not just what the competitor should do in the arena but also where to give the marks. Some find this easy, but aids for those who do not include diagrammatic representations of the test and even using your carpet as an arena and walking, trotting and cantering through the test yourself.

ON THE DAY

Arrive in plenty of time, a minimum of a quarter of an hour before the class as there will be plenty to do including:

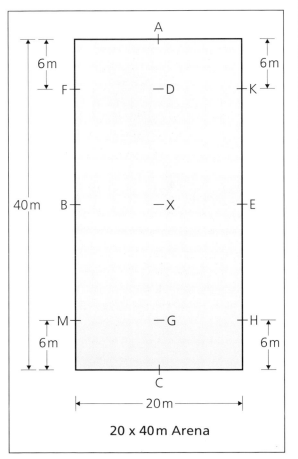

20 x 40m Arena

- Finding the secretary, your arena and your writer.
- Checking the arena (the boards, letters and centre line), establishing if any special rules apply (no whips, entry from outside the arena or inside etc).
- Checking your tools (a pen, a bell or horn) and, if in a car, whether the windscreen is clean.

- Briefing the writer as to how you like the sheet completed.
- Most importantly, start to focus on the test. I like to run through the whole test in my mind, develop a feeling for a rhythm to the assessment and be really prepared so that the first rider does not get meaner marks than his rivals.

THE WAY OF GOING

It is relatively straightforward to assess the technical requirements such as a square halt or whether a transition was at C, but these are only part of the picture. It is the way of going, how the horse does the movements, that really exposes whether the horse has been well trained and is not merely obedient.

With the movements the judge should be looking at not just whether the technical requirements are achieved but also the way they are achieved. In each and every movement it helps to ask yourself if the horse kept:

- **RHYTHM**
- **SUPPLENESS**
- **CONTACT**
- **IMPULSION**
- **STRAIGHTNESS**

These five goals are known as the scales (as in piano not fish) of training and at more advanced levels collection is added as the sixth. Together with self-carriage they are the ingredients for quality work and a good way of going.

ATHLETIC ABILITY

Dressage is much more than achieving the technical requirements of a movement. Equally, if not more, important is the way the horse performs the movements; that indicates whether a horse has been trained to be an athlete, and is not simply going through the motions.

RHYTHM

The rhythm to the gaits should be regular. This means that the rhythm should be both correct for each gait and repeated with a constant tempo (speed of the rhythm).

Correct rhythm *The walk* is a marching four-time gait so there are equal intervals between each step. Often when a horse gets tense this four-time rhythm is lost and at times gets so bad that the rhythm becomes two-time with the legs moving in lateral pairs (pacing). This is a serious fault marked down in the movement and the collective marks.

The trot is a two-time gait with the legs moving in diagonal pairs and with a moment of suspension between them. Most horses keep this two-time rhythm and the more common fault is that they have little or no suspension.

The canter is a three-time gait with a clear moment of suspension and with a particular leading leg. Many horses lose the three-time rhythm when they are slowed up and do not maintain impulsion. Some develop a flat canter without a clear moment of suspension.

Tempo It is important for the rider to find a speed at which the horse shows off the gaits to their best. Many riders rush their horses around the arena and some take them so slowly they have no impulsion. When found, this tempo needs to be regular, i.e. no speeding up or slowing down; this is particularly difficult and important when lengthening the strides.

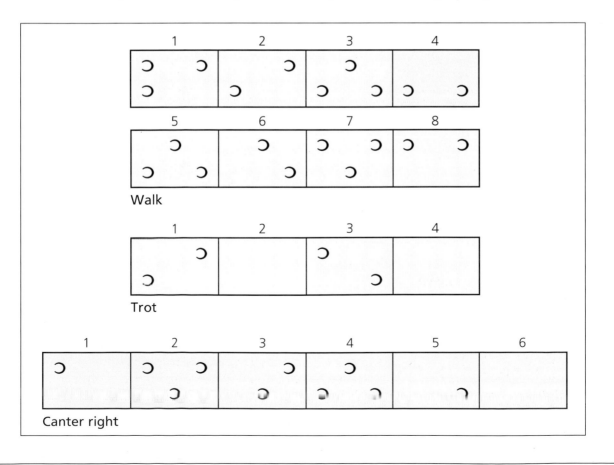

Walk

Trot

Canter right

SUPPLENESS

The supple horse has 'let go' of the tension in his muscles, his joints are loose and he does not tighten his body and resist the rider's aids.

The muscles that need to be particularly supple are those over the top line from the hind legs over the quarters, loins, in front of the withers and up to the poll.

The test of whether the horse is supple and 'letting go' over his back and neck is that, when the contact is eased, as in the free-rein walk, trot or canter the horse wants to stretch forward and down (*right*) and not, as is so often the case, upward.

He has to be supple enough to bend along the line of the circle or corner (*above*). This bend should be equal in both directions and be maintained evenly along the length of his body, not just a neck bend (*above*).

CONTACT

The contact to aim for is a light, even, elastic feel in both reins and this is achieved by aids from the legs, not the hands. The legs are applied as a driving aid, the horse steps under his body more with his hind legs and works 'through' those muscles along his top line – over the back and neck – and the rider feels the energy thus created in the reins. The horse's outline and steps will be 'round' not hollow and flat.

Judges need to ensure that the rein contact is both consistent and elastic without the horse leaning and balancing on it, and that the rider is not pulling back but providing a forward tendency to the contact. If the contact is made with the rider's hands rather than the seat and legs the horse's neck will tend to shorten and compress. An arched neck is an important indicator of a correct way of going.

A good contact produces an arched neck (*top*), and not a shortened neck (*middle*) or an overbent one (*bottom*).

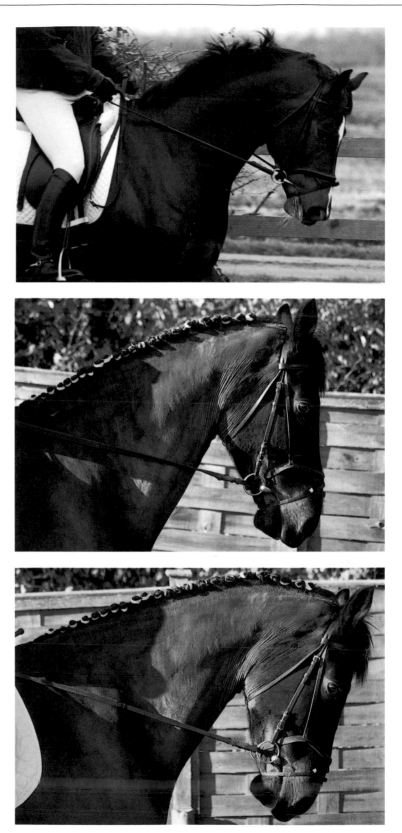

IMPULSION

This is the power of the horse and comes from the activity of the hindquarters with the hind legs taking active steps that swing forward under the body in the moment of suspension in the trot and canter. The impulsion is contained by the rein contact which prevents the horse from using up this extra energy to simply go faster. Any resistance, tightening of muscles, ligaments and joints, will block this energy getting through so the horse must be supple to be able to build up real impulsion.

A good rider will create enough impulsion to show off his horse's athleticism but not so much that it cannot be controlled.

Impulsion being clearly developed in the hindquarters at the trot (*below*) and canter (*right*).

STRAIGHTNESS

Horses, like humans, are born one sided and will tend to move forward with their bodies slightly curved. This crookedness can get worse if a rider sits to one side and/or keeps a stronger contact with one rein than the other. When a horse is crooked it will be more difficult for him to stay balanced, to build up impulsion and to have an even contact.

The hind legs should step into the tracks of the forelegs (*below left*) both on a straight line and on a circle. Often the horse's hindquarters slip to one side (*below*) and, although this is excusable with a young horse, it becomes a serious fault as the tests and training advance.

THE MOVEMENTS

The more important mark earners and losers are noted for novice level movements.

FREE WALK ON A LONG REIN

Mark earners

THE RIDER:

- gives the horse the freedom to stretch forward and down;
- maintains a very very light contact.

THE HORSE:

- takes long free strides with clear over-tracking (hind feet stepping in front of the hoof prints of the forefeet);
- marches purposefully forward;
- uses all of his body so his muscles are rippling and are not tight;
- has a clear four-time rhythm.

Mark losers

THE HORSE:

snatches at the reins; raises the head, does not stretch down; takes short steps; holds back and lacks energy; quickens and tends to rush. Intervals between hoof beats become unequal.

THE RIDER:

releases so much contact that it is a loose rein (*top right*); keeps the contact so much that it restricts the horse's freedom to stretch down.

MEDIUM WALK

Mark earners

THE RIDER:

- keeps a contact allowing the head to be on/or in front of the vertical

THE HORSE:

- marches purposefully forward with steps that overtrack;

- has a supple and unconstrained body, particularly through the back;
- has a rhythm in the correct sequence.

Mark losers

THE HORSE:

holds back not stepping forward towards the bit; has uneven steps; loses the correct sequence (when the sequence is correct at a stage during the stride the lateral pairs of legs form a V [*below*]); is tight and resists; takes short steps.

WORKING TROT

This is the trot in which the young horse finds it easiest to keep his balance with the strides being neither as short as in the collected trot or as long as in the medium trot.

A good working trot should be in balance and with active steps (*top*) but if balance and carriage are not so good the horse might fall onto the forehand (*below*).

Mark earners

THE HORSE:

- works forward to a light elastic contact;
- keeps a good tempo, neither speeding up nor slowing down;
- takes active steps with the hind legs showing good hock action and swinging clearly forward in the moment of suspension;
- has a supple and swinging back so the tail swings from side to side;
- takes elastic steps and there is a spring to them;
- has free, unconstrained strides with a clear moment of suspension;
- has a regular rhythm and even steps.

Mark losers

THE HORSE:

leans on or draws back or above the contact; tends to speed up and slow down; lacks activity in the hind legs and tends to drag them along; does not swing through the back; falls onto the forehand and does not take enough weight on the hindquarters; pokes the nose out with a rather stiff neck; is short in the neck and/or overbends; takes stiff and inactive steps; strides show little or no suspension; holds back; tightens; has strides showing so much suspension that the trot is close to a passage.

WORKING CANTER

This corresponds to the working trot and is therefore the variation of canter between collected canter and medium canter in which the horse finds it easiest to keep his balance.

Mark earners
THE HORSE:
- maintains a three-time rhythm with a defined moment of suspension;
- takes springy and light steps;
- has a well-marked cadence (a pronounced rhythm);
- has active hind legs showing a good hock action;
- maintains the tempo;
- is straight whether on a straight line or following the line of a circle;
- stays on the required leading leg with the correct sequence;
- gives the appearance of the strides being uphill (*below*).

Mark losers
THE HORSE:
loses the three-time rhythm; has flat strides with little or no suspension; is on the forehand; has stiff hock action; does not step under the weight with the hind legs; speeds up and/or slows down; has his hindquarters drifting in or out; canters disunited.

LENGTHENED STRIDES

Mark earners
THE HORSE:
- makes a progressive transition from the working gait into the lengthened strides and when returning to the working gait;
- maintains the tempo not just in the lengthened strides but also in the transitions into and from them;
- shows a clear increased length to the strides from the working trot (*below*) or working canter (*opposite top*);

- keeps balance and self-carriage;
- keeps swinging through his back and does not tighten it;
- maintains the rhythm;
- remains straight.

Mark losers

THE HORSE:

speeds up into the lengthening and slows down when returning to the working gait; loses balance with a change of tempo in the lengthening; does not really lengthen the steps; runs onto the forehand; tightens and resists; becomes irregular; tends to flick the forelegs in the trot; has inactive hind legs which are not generating the impulsion.

KEEPING THE TEMPO

In the canter the horse usually finds it easier to keep the tempo and avoid speeding up and slowing down but finds it much more difficult to stay straight.

GIVE AND RETAKE THE REINS

The rider pushes both hands forward to release and then retake the contact. This movement of the hands should be continuous so there is no need for them to stay forward with the released contact.

Mark earners

THE RIDER:

- shows a clear release of contact with both reins.

THE HORSE:

- stays in the same tempo and keeps balanced;
- maintains the same outline or, if anything, stretches a little forward and down.

Mark losers

THE RIDER:

does not really release the contact and may do this by lifting their hands as they put them forward (*above*) or by keeping the contact with the rein the judge cannot see.

THE HORSE:

stiffens; hollows and lifts his head; speeds up or slows down.

COUNTER CANTER

The horse canters with the outside leg leading.

Mark earners

THE HORSE:

- stays flexed in the direction of the leading leg.

Other mark earners are as for Working Canter on page 14.

Mark losers

THE HORSE:

- bends in the direction of the turn. Other mark losers are as for Working Canter on page 14.

THE REIN BACK

Mark earners

THE RIDER:

- establishes the halt before reining back.

THE HORSE:

- steps back the required distance or number of steps;
- moves back with diagonal pairs of hind and forelegs being lifted at the same time;
- steps actively;
- stays supple and submissive;
- is always ready to move forward;
- steps back straight;
- maintains self-carriage which is particularly difficult to keep in this movement.

Mark losers

THE HORSE:

anticipates the aids and rushes back; takes too many or too few steps; loses the correct sequence (*below*); drags the legs back; goes wide behind; tightens or resists; drifts to one side with the hind legs; does not move forward on the aids.

THE TRANSITIONS

Previously transitions were judged as just part of a movement but, because they are so important, they now often have a mark to themselves. In the transition any short-comings are shown up because for the horse to stay in balance during a transition he needs to have rhythm, suppleness, contact, impulsion, straightness and the start of collection. The ability of the horse to collect in the future is shown by how easy he finds it to step under the body in the downward transitions (from lengthened strides to the working gaits, to the halt etc), and take the weight backward onto his hindquarters. One of the most common faults in transitions is that impulsion is lost in the downward transitions within a gait: when coming down from the lengthened strides to the working gait, the rider slows the horse down with the reins and does not keep the same activity and energy as was shown when lengthening.

The photos opposite and on the following page show good and bad transitions. A good trot-walk transition helps to engage the horse (1, 2, 3).

See page 18 for the following examples: Holding back in this transition to the canter has led to a loss of balance (4). A more advanced horse in a transition from canter to walk (5, 6). A trot-walk transition (7, 8).

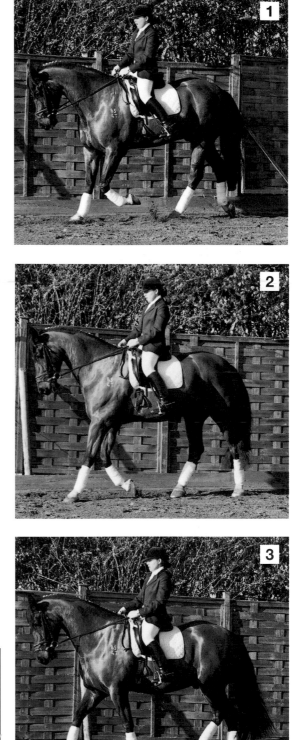

TRANSITION QUALITY

The transitions are the best indicators of the quality of the training and dressage tests are putting increasing emphasis on them.

Mark earners

- For the novice horse the quality of the transition is more important than the accuracy, but the higher the level of the test the more important it is to complete the transition at the prescribed marker.
- At preliminary, novice and elementary levels the transition through two gaits (trot to halt, canter to walk) can be progressive and show steps of the middle gait, but at medium level and above the transition should be direct.
- The transition is defined so there is no confusion as to where it starts and ends.
- The cadence of the gait is maintained up to the moment of the gait change so there is no difference in the quality of the steps.
- The tempo of the gait is the same up to the moment of the gait change and, if within a gait, is the same all the time.

There is no speeding up in the upward transitions and no slowing down in the downward transitions.

Mark losers

THE HORSE:

is not on the aids and the transition is very late or very early; changes tempo (when the transition is within a gait the tempo should remain constant all the time and when it is from one gait to another it is constant up to the time of change); does not step further under his body in the downward transitions, does not stay engaged in upward transitions; loses any of the scales of training.

THE HALT

The halt is expected to improve as a horse matures and advances in his training. This is a good halt for a young horse (*below*).

This horse, who is a little more advanced, demonstrates a very good halt (*left*). Here the novice horse has executed a halt that lacks engagement and is not square (*below, left*).

Mark earners

THE HORSE:

- ideally, should stand four square but a novice that has little engagement of the hindquarters can leave one hind leg slightly behind;
- has the forelegs as a pair abreast of each other;
- stands still, attentive and ready to move off;
- performs a good transition (see page 17) into the halt stepping under the weight to come into as engaged a halt as is suitable for the stage of training;
- performs a good transition (see page 17) from the halt moving forward willingly.

Mark losers

THE HORSE:

does not engage the hindquarters into the halt; falls onto the forehand; loses self-carriage; swings the hindquarters or holds them to one side; is restless and does not stay in a halt; performs poor transitions in or out of the halt; loses balance; hollows or overbends.

THE FIGURES

THE CIRCLE

Mark earners

- The shape of the circle must be correct with the horse always on a curve and his body bent to follow the line of the curvature.

- The size of the circle must be correct although, with a novice horse, a metre more or less is of little concern if the quality of the trot or canter is good.

Mark losers

THE HORSE:

shows too much bend and his weight falls on to the outside shoulder; is bent to the outside; has his hindquarters drifting in or out; tilts; loses the quality of the gait.

TURNS

When making a turn in the corners of the arena a horse in working trot should complete the arc of a quarter of a circle of about 8 m diameter. In collected trot the diameter should be 6 m.

Mark earners and losers

As for the circle.

SERPENTINES

The serpentine is a series of loops made up of half circles connected by straight lines. As the horse crosses the centre line he should be parallel to the short side.

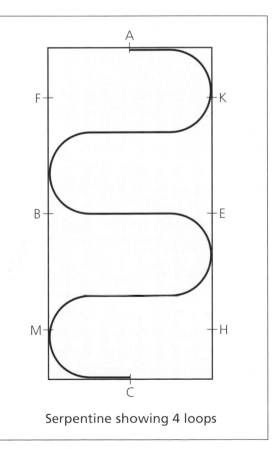

Serpentine showing 4 loops

Mark earners

THE HORSE:

- should have a clearly established bend through his whole body following the line of the half circle;
- is straightened across the centre line and the new bend of the new loop should be clearly established;
- should have equal bend, quality of steps and tempo on both reins.
- When on the half circles the mark earners are the same as for the circle.

THE COLLECTIVE MARKS

These assess the overall picture of a test and, roughly, the horse's ability is assessed in the gaits mark, how well he has been trained is assessed in the impulsion and submission marks and how he has been ridden is assessed in the rider mark.

THE GAITS

Assessment points

Their regularity: the rhythm of the sequence should be correct for the walk, trot and canter with the steps being level.

Their freedom: the horse should be able to cover the ground, to lengthen his strides and to use his whole body (*top right*).

IMPULSION

Assessment points

The desire to go forward: the eagerness and ability of the horse to work forward.

The suppleness of the back: the horse's back should swing and there should be no tight-

ness or resistance stopping the forward momentum getting through.

The elasticity of the steps: there should be a spring to the steps, the joints should be mobile and the hind legs used to help generate the power and expression that are the hallmarks of impulsion (*below*).

The engagement of the hindquarters: the hind legs should step under the body and generate the power.

SUBMISSION

Assessment points

Attention and confidence: the horse willingly does what the rider asks.

Harmony, lightness and ease of movements: the horse finds it within his ability to do what is asked and works well with the rider.

Acceptance of the bit: the horse keeps that light elastic contact with the bit and works in an easy self-carriage (*top right*).

Lightness of the forehand: the horse, according to the level of the test, should be carrying enough weight on the hindquarters to do the test movements with ease.

THE RIDER

Assessment points

The position and the seat: whether it is balanced and correct (*right*).

The correctness and effectiveness of the aids: whether the aids are applied correctly and what effect they have on the horse.

ACKNOWLEDGEMENTS

I should like to express my thanks to all those who helped me in the preparation of this book. Carrie Anne McGregor and Henriette Anderson who were such good guinea pigs for the photographs, being skilled enough to perform movements both well and badly at my request; Bula Brazil who checked the manuscript, and the judges, riders, trainers, books and FEI Directives that have helped me acquire my knowledge of judging. Finally and far from least there have been the horses who, whether I have been riding, training or judging them, have been very special teachers. I also wish to thank Kevin Sparrow for the lower photo on page 23.

British Library Cataloguing-in-Publication Data.
A catalogue record for this book is available from the British Library

ISBN 0.85131.817.7

Published in Great Britain in 2001 by
J. A. Allen an imprint of Robert Hale Ltd.,
Clerkenwell House, 45–47 Clerkenwell Green,
London EC1R 0HT

Reprinted 2002

Design and Typesetting by Paul Saunders
Series editor Jane Lake
Colour processing by Tenon & Polert Colour Processing Ltd., Hong Kong
Printed in Malta by Gutenberg Press Ltd.